WITHDRAWN

★ HOCKEY SUPERSTARS ★

CAREY PRICE

BY MATT DOEDEN

CAPSTONE PRESS
a capstone imprint

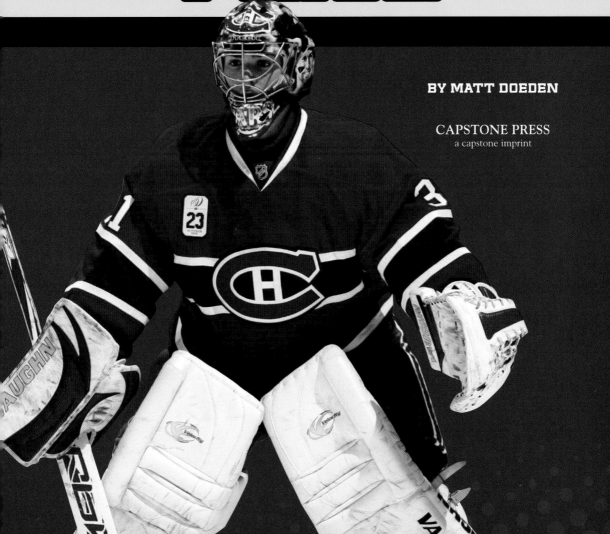

Sports Illustrated Kids Hockey Superstars are published by Capstone Press,
1710 Roe Crest Drive, North Mankato, Minnesota 56003.
www.capstonepub.com

Library of Congress Cataloging-in-Publication Data
Doeden, Matt.
Carey Price / by Matt Doeden.
pages cm. – (Sports Illustrated Kids. Hockey Superstars.)
Includes bibliographical references and index.
Summary: "Details the life and career of hockey superstar Carey Price"— Provided
by publisher.
Audience: Age: 9-15.
Audience: Grade: 4 to 6.
ISBN 978-1-4914-2140-6 (library binding)
1. Price, Carey, 1987—Juvenile literature. 2. Hockey players—Canada—Biography—
Juvenile literature. I. Title.
GV848.5.P75D64 2015
796.962092—dc23
[B]   2014026394

Editorial Credits
Brenda Haugen, editor; Ted Williams, designer; Eric Gohl, media researcher;
Morgan Walters, production specialist

Photo Credits
AP Photo: Bradley C Bower, 12; Dreamstime: Jerry Coli, 23; Getty Images: Chris
Relke, 10, NHL/Dave Sandford, 13, Richard Wolowicz, 9; Newscom: Icon SMI/Minas
Panagiotakis, 26–27; Sports Illustrated: Damian Strohmeyer, cover, 1, 14, 20–21, 30–31
(background), 32 (background), David E. Klutho, back cover, 7, 17, 19, 25, 29, Robert
Beck, 4–5

Design Elements:
Shutterstock

Printed in the United States of America in Stevens Point, Wisconsin.
092014   008479WZS15

TABLE OF CONTENTS

CHAPTER 1

SHUTTING THE DOOR

The crowd was on its feet for the 2014 Olympic men's hockey semi-final game. The United States and Canada battled for the right to go to the gold-medal match. Team Canada was clinging to a 1-0 lead late in the third period.

Carey Price, a 26-year-old goalie from Canada, stood in front of the net. Price had been nearly perfect during the entire Winter Olympics. Now he faced a desperate Team USA. The Americans charged time and again. But Canada's smothering defense fought them off. When the Americans did get a shot away, Price was there to make the save.

With just under a minute to play, Team USA had the puck in Canada's zone. Center Joe Pavelski grabbed a loose puck in front of the goal and fired off a quick slapshot. But once again Price was there. The goaltender knocked it away for a teammate to collect. It was the 31st shot Price had faced in the game. He stopped all 31, and Canada held on for a 1-0 victory.

Canada then faced Sweden for the gold medal. Canada led 1-0 in the second period. Sweden blasted a series of shots at Price, but they couldn't get one by him. Then a shot was deflected on its way toward the goal. The puck took a sudden change of direction. It looked like a sure goal for Sweden.

But Price was ready. He dove across the goal and snatched the puck out of the air with his glove. It was probably his greatest save of the tournament. Sweden never got another chance that good, and Canada went on to win 3-0. They were the gold medalists! Price had posted back-to-back **shutouts**. The International Ice Hockey Federation named him the most valuable goaltender of the tournament.

shutout—when a team doesn't score

FAST FACT

During his five games at the 2014 Winter Olympics, Price allowed only three goals.

CHAPTER 2

EARLY LIFE

Carey was born August 16, 1987, in British Columbia, Canada, to Lynda and Jerry Price. He grew up in the small town of Anahim Lake, British Columbia.

Carey's father loved hockey. Jerry had been **drafted** as a goaltender by the Philadelphia Flyers in the late 1970s. He never played a National Hockey League (NHL) game, but Jerry did pass his love of the game on to his son. Because Anahim Lake didn't have a hockey arena, Carey learned to play on a nearby frozen creek.

By age 9 Carey was showing talent for the game, but there were no organized **leagues** near the Price home. So a few days a week, Jerry and Carey drove about four hours to Williams Lake so Carey could join a team.

draft—the process of choosing a person to join a sports organization or team

league—a group of sports teams that play against each other

FAST FACT

Carey's mother is a Native Canadian. She served as the chief

Jerry Price (left) accepted the Goalie of the Year award on behalf of his son, Carey, at the 2007 Canadian Hockey League awards banquet.

All that driving was tiring for Carey and his dad. So Jerry learned to fly and bought a small plane. By air the trip from Anahim Lake to Williams Lake took less than an hour.

Carey was one of the top **amateur** goalies in Canada by 2002. It was time to step up to the Canadian Hockey League (CHL), one of the world's top amateur leagues. The Tri-City Americans picked Price in the league's draft. The 16-year-old left his home, his family, and his country, to travel to Pasco, Washington, where the Americans were based.

At first Carey didn't play much. Many of the other CHL players were older. But by his second season, Carey was getting regular playing time. He made the most of it, leading the Americans to victory in their opening playoff series.

amateur—athlete who is not paid for playing a sport

JUNIOR HOCKEY

Most of Canada's top teenage players hone their skills in junior leagues, which are all led by the CHL. The CHL includes 60 teams in Canada and the United States. To keep teams balanced, the teams draft the top players. That's why players such as Price often have to travel far from home— even to another country—to play junior hockey.

NHL scouts were taking notice. By 2005 he was one of the top goaltending prospects in North America. The Montreal Canadiens picked him fifth overall in the 2005 NHL Draft. Still Price continued to play for the Americans. He had a record of 30-13-1 and was named the CHL goaltender of the year in 2006–07.

Finally, in 2007, Price joined the Hamilton Bulldogs of the American Hockey League (AHL). The Bulldogs are a minor league team for the Canadiens. The Bulldogs' regular season was just ending when Price arrived. He played just two games during

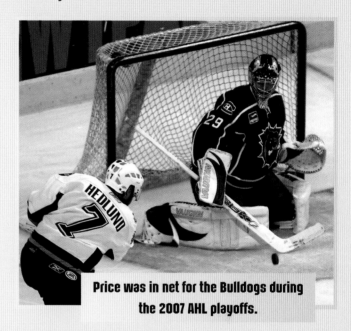

Price was in net for the Bulldogs during the 2007 AHL playoffs.

the regular season and won them both. Then Price led the Bulldogs to an amazing playoff run. They won the AHL championship, called the Calder Cup. Price was named the **most valuable player** (MVP) of the playoffs!

most valuable player—an honor given to the best player each season

Price was the fifth overall pick in the NHL Draft.

CHAPTER 3

NHL HIGHS AND LOWS

Price was named to the Canadiens' NHL roster in 2007. At age 20 he started his first game in Pittsburgh against the Penguins. The high-scoring Penguins were one of the league's top teams, but Price was ready for the challenge. The **rookie** stopped 26 of the 28 shots he faced, and Montreal won 3-2.

In February Price earned the first shutout of his career in a 1-0 victory against the Philadelphia Flyers. Soon after Montreal traded starting goaltender Cristobal Huet. Price was Montreal's new number one goalie!

He didn't disappoint. Price helped Montreal to the playoffs. They faced the Boston Bruins in the first round. The series went to a winner-take-all Game 7. Price was at his best. He stopped all 25 Boston shots for a shutout and a 5-0 victory. Montreal lost the next round to the Flyers, but it had been a great first season for Price. He was named to the NHL's All-Rookie First Team.

rookie—a first-year player

Price entered the 2008–09 season with great expectations. The 21-year-old started out red hot. He won seven of his first 10 games. That included a 4-0 shutout of the Ottawa Senators on November 11.

Everything changed when Price injured his ankle during a game against the Tampa Bay Lightning December 30. He missed almost a month of play and struggled to return to form. The Canadiens won just seven games and lost 20 down the stretch. The playoffs proved to be just as difficult. The Bruins swept the Canadiens in the first round. Price allowed 15 goals in those four games.

THE BUTTERFLY

Price uses his hockey instincts and quick reactions in a goaltending style called the butterfly. Early in the NHL's history, most goaltenders used a simple stand-up style. They stayed on their feet as much as possible. In the 1960s goaltenders such as Tony Esposito began to fall to their knees to stop low shots. Some people thought they looked like butterflies with their arms and legs out to the side of the body.

The stand-up style continued to dominate the league during the 1970s. That began to change in the 1980s. Goaltender Patrick Roy perfected the butterfly style. He enjoyed great success with his updated style, and others took notice. The butterfly soon became the most popular goaltending style. Many of today's top goalies, including Price, use it.

THE MONTREAL CANADIENS

The Montreal Canadiens are one of the oldest and most successful teams in NHL history. The Canadiens were one of the original members of the NHL, which formed in 1917. The Canadiens won their first **Stanley Cup** in 1916 when they were part of the National Hockey Association. Since then the team has won 24 Stanley Cups, more than any team in history.

Price's second-half struggles carried into the 2009–10 season. In the third game, Price allowed seven goals against the Vancouver Canucks.

It was just the beginning of a difficult season. By the end of the season, Price had lost his starting job to Jaroslav Halak. With Halak in goal, the team was able to find success. The Canadiens made a great playoff run all the way to the Eastern Conference Final. Price barely played during

the playoffs, and when he did, he continued
to struggle.

    In just a year and a half, Price had gone
from rising star to benchwarmer. Fans
wondered about his future. Both he and Halak
were free agents. Montreal decided to keep
the younger Price. He signed a two-year,
$5.5 million contract to return to the team.

Stanley Cup—the
trophy given each year
to the NHL champion

free agent—a player
who is free to sign with
any team

In 2010–11 Price proved that the Canadiens had made the right choice. He was better than ever. His 38 wins were tied for the most in the league. He posted a career-high eight shutouts and was named to the All-Star Team.

The Canadiens returned to the playoffs with high hopes. They faced the Boston Bruins in the opening round. Montreal took control, winning the first two games in Boston by a

Price appeared in 72 games for Montreal in 2010–11. That was the most for a goaltender in team history.

combined score of 5-1. Price was dominant in goal. However, beginning with Game 3, it all fell apart. The team struggled to score, and Price was under fire. In Game 5, he faced a stunning 51 shots. He stopped all but two of them. Yet even that wasn't enough, as the Bruins won 2-1. Boston won four of the last five games to advance and end Montreal's season.

The 2011–12 season was disappointing for Price and the Canadiens. Price was unable to match his great play of the previous season. The team won just 31 games and missed the playoffs. Yet after the season, Montreal gave the 24-year-old Price a new six-year contract worth $39 million.

A labor dispute between owners and players marked the start of the 2012–13 season. The owners announced a **lockout**. It appeared the season might be cancelled, but the sides came to a last-minute agreement. The shortened season began in January.

Price and the Canadiens enjoyed a great regular season. They had the second-best record in the Eastern Conference and cruised into the playoffs. They faced the Ottawa Senators in the first round. It was a tight series until late in Game 4. Price had to leave the ice with a lower body injury. He never returned, and Ottawa went on to win the series.

lockout—a period of time in which owners prevent players from reporting to their teams; owners do not pay players during lockouts and no games are played

Price's life was in for big changes in 2013–14. Before the NHL season, Price married his longtime girlfriend, Angela Webber. The couple had been dating since they were teenagers.

During the 2013–14 season, Price was selected to represent Canada at the 2014 Winter Olympics in Sochi, Russia. Heading into the games, some hockey experts said Team Canada lacked a dominant goaltender. Nobody even knew for sure who would be the main starter. Canada coach Mike Babcock answered that question by putting Price in the net for the team's opening game. Price stepped up to the task, earning a 3-1 victory against Norway.

Price's quick reflexes, combined with Canada's strong defensive style, made him almost unbeatable. Over five games he posted an amazing **save percentage** of .972. That included his back-to-back shutouts in the semi-final against the United States and the gold medal match against Sweden.

save percentage—a statistic that measures the percentage of shots a goaltender stops

Latvia's Lauris Darzins scored the only goal against Price in Team Canada's 2-1 semi-final victory.

Price was still on top of his game when he returned to Montreal to resume the NHL season. Price collected 34 wins on the season. His .927 save percentage was among the best in the NHL.

Price was brilliant in the playoffs as well. He and the Canadiens swept the Tampa Bay Lightning in the first round. Montreal fell behind Boston three games to two in the second round. Then Price allowed just one goal in the next two games combined to lead the Canadiens to the Eastern Conference Finals.

The New York Rangers jumped out to a 2-0 lead early in the first game. In the second period, Rangers forward Chris Kreider took off on a breakaway. He drove toward the net and crashed hard into Price. The goaltender's leg slammed into the goal post. Price tried to stay in the game, but his leg was injured. He soon had to come out, and he never returned. Price had to watch from the bench as the Rangers knocked Montreal out of the hunt for the Stanley Cup, four games to two.

CHAPTER 4

THE FUTURE

Carey Price's Olympic success made him a household name in Canada. It's a country that views hockey as a national pastime, and Price's play made him a hero to many people.

Yet the sudden attention seemed to have little effect on Price. Even after celebrating his gold medal with his teammates, he never lost his focus. He won six of his first seven starts after returning from Russia.

At just 26 years old, Price has already seen plenty of hockey highs and lows. But his natural talent has always been there. He's proven his value in the regular season. He's won it all at the Olympics. The next step, his fans hope, is winning a Stanley Cup.

GLOSSARY

amateur (AM-uh-chur)—athlete who is not paid for playing a sport

draft (DRAFT)—the process of choosing a person to join a sports organization or team

free agent (FREE AY-juhnt)—a player who is free to sign with any team

league (LEEG)—a group of sports teams that play against each other

lockout (LOK-out)—a period of time in which owners prevent players from reporting to their teams; owners do not pay players during lockouts and no games are played

most valuable player (MOHST VAL-yoo-buhl PLAY-ur)—an honor given to the best player each season

rookie (RUK-ee)—a first-year player

save percentage (SAYV pur-SEN-tayj)—a statistic that measures the percentage of shots a goaltender stops

shutout (SHUHT-out)—when a team doesn't score

Stanley Cup (STAN-lee KUP)—the trophy given each year to the NHL champion

READ MORE

Doeden, Matt. *Sidney Crosby: Hockey Superstar.* Sports Illustrated Kids: Superstar Athletes. Mankato, Minn.: Capstone Press, 2012.

Frederick, Shane. *The Ultimate Guide to Pro Hockey Teams.* Sports Illustrated Kids: Ultimate Pro Team Guides. Mankato, Minn.: Capstone Press, 2011.

Gitlin, Marty. *Hockey.* Best Sport Ever. Minneapolis: ABDO Pub., 2012.

INTERNET SITES

FactHound offers a safe, fun way to find Internet sites related to this book. All of the sites on FactHound have been researched by our staff.

Here's all you do:

Visit *www.facthound.com*

Type in this code: 9781491421406

Super-cool stuff!

Check out projects, games and lots more at
www.capstonekids.com

INDEX